ANALYZE ME

WHAT'S YOUR INTERPRETATION?

JOHN EDWARD FARMER

Order this book online at www.trafford.com
or email orders@trafford.com

Most Trafford titles are also available at major online book retailers.

Printed in the United States of America.

ISBN: 978-1-4669-8632-9 (sc)
ISBN: 978-1-4669-8634-3 (hc)
ISBN: 978-1-4669-8633-6 (e)

Library of Congress Control Number: 2013904911

Trafford rev. 03/19/2013

 www.trafford.com

North America & international
toll-free: 1 888 232 4444 (USA & Canada)
phone: 250 383 6864 ♦ fax: 812 355 4082

CONTENTS

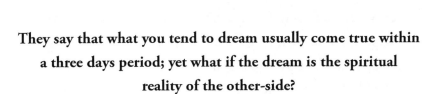

They say that what you tend to dream usually come true within a three days period; yet what if the dream is the spiritual reality of the other-side?

Dreams are considered a supernatural communication, whose message(s) could be unraveled by people; Yet in modern times, various schools of psychology have offered theories about the meaning of dreams.

January 02

Out and about enjoying the weather; Sun bright, the wind is calm. Everything seems perfect. Behind me on the left was an apartment building, but more like a house with a store across from it—that is separated by a sidewalk.

For some reason I heard a sound—like a blow-horn. I ask those around me—"did you hear that?" But no one respond back. For some reason I look up and from yonder, there were a length of unbreakable clouds—it had to be at least two (2) miles long, maybe a half a mile wide and in the beginning of the cloud on both side, I could see a soldier with a staff of some sort of symbol (a golden crest). On the outside of the soldiers were hippos, all four standing looking forward like statues; yet standing still and moving as if they were on an escalator—gliding across the sky.

So then I yell out—to get inside, as I head in my car; roll the window up, as the drop of 'Black-oil like rain' begins to fall. As the black rain hit the ground and I'm trying to contact my mother and brother—who are in the house, Cell-Phones begin to go haywire—Try speed dialing and multiple numbers would appear. The whole computer systems shut down.

What's Your Interpretation?

JANUARY 03

M e and a friend were preparing to head down South—for whatever reason, I don't know; maybe just traveling around the States. So we stop at our old neighborhood, which the street is now control by three (3) different types of gang members. The rules were if you were not part of one of the gangs—you would be whip or thrown in the school (which now below in the basement-part were like a prison). My friend and I had stop and slip into my old apartment (which now does not look nothing like Rockaway Beach) there my mother and brother fixing dinner. I told my friend, "It would be best to leave in the morning; at least we may have a better chance to get out". So I told my mother the same.

As the morning break-in, there a female lying next to me and we are the only two (2) in this huge bed, so I make my move onto her, but at the same time listening out for anyone that may come into the room. While we are lying sideway, I thrust myself into her petite body and she spoke out a quick "um!" which ring throughout the house. She releases herself and I got up to get dress. So we pack our bag and a lady stated to us the best way to get out of the Project and to reach dad's other house; which was through the school and across the yard. So we begin our journey.

As we walk through and sneaking around corner to get to the other end, the bell ring . . . then another bell ring (like a buzzing sound). That is when we knew we need to hide—fast. So, we snuck downstairs (which is not a good idea at the time) into the bathroom and another fellow stated, "for them not to do any harm . . . you have to urine on yourself and on most part of your body". So we did, got in the stall and splash my urine across my chest and arm. When the coast were clear, we heard on out through the back to cross the field. There one of the leader, begin to hit me across the chest and face with a paddle and as he swipe from an upward and down across me, I could feel the strike, but no mark on my body. So they grab me up to take me back toward the school, but I escape, and my friend and I ran toward my father's house.

There he stood and open the door for us to get in. Then while closing the door, he stated, "I saw you both coming"; with a bat-like object in his hand. He slightly open the door and the head-leader threw a rubber-ball with an elastic attach to it toward the door, and my father, caught the ball with his right hand and the gang leader tried to pull the elastic ball back, as we look down at him, as he disappear to my left behind the tree. My father pulled as much on the elastic-rubber-band-like-ball and let it go with such force, that it kills the leader. The other member yell out, "you kill him", then a wolf-like dog came running up toward the step and I quickly shut the door and ensure all four (4) locks were bolted. (For some reason—the gang members seem to be afraid of coming up to people's steps). The banging from the dog stops for a few second and begin again, but this time the door bend in the corner. Got a stick to tried to poke the nose of the dog, the dog kept coming through and I soon recognizes it wasn't the dog this time, but my dog (Butch); who had chase the other dogs away. Thank you, Butch.

What's Your Interpretation?

_____

_____

_____

_____

_____

_____

_____

_____

_____

_____

_____

_____

_____

_____

_____

_____

_____

_____

_____

_____

_____

JANUARY 06

We're heading to a church; the weather were fine, sun out . . . many of those I know from the choirs and friend (i.e. mostly from the old neighborhood) had pull up in some type of luxury vehicle, and a female park next to me as we both had our vehicles park rear-end first. We begin to talk of how it been a long time since we saw each other. So we both got out, head over to a picnic table and begin to talk some more. Before we gather our belonging, I sort of place my hand underneath her jawbone and place a kiss on her lip. Then a mass of crowd begin to head inside the church. The female, I was chatting with (didn't even know her name), but we had met before. As my other friends gather around, there were a few that didn't take like in me; as if I had done something bad to them. So as we or most of us perceive to head inside, there I see my best friends (Leonard, Julie, Mykell, Arthur, my brother (when he was younger); mom who kept telling us to hurry to get a seat up front. I ask my brother how is things and my mother stated, "He still looking for work". So I stated to him to send me his resume and I can get him a job with me at the hospital.

As we deciding where to sit, the pastor calls out my name to sit in the pulpit; but I was unsure. While in the back of the church the choirs begin to march in singing, 'We come this far by Faith'. I turn to my left and there my father sitting near the side, but the last four seat were facing the aisle, in which only two (2) people can sit in each row. So my brother, one of his buddies from the usher and myself sat in one of the seat.

Yet in the beginning, at a house an uncle came over, because he was passing through. During the stay, my brother had just come in from upstairs to join with my father and mother along with my aunt.

My uncle or stranger came in through the kitchen which were part of the bedroom and pour some of my good liquor called 'Cross Keys' a Barbados Rum. It angers me because he didn't ask me if he could have a taste. So I went to sleep, then minutes later my brother were about to pour some more for the stranger, as he ask me, "can uncle have some?" I stated to him, "he may have some of the Bacardi 151 only and not the other", my "uncle" requested the other drink and I gave him an ultimatum, than I stated, "You get none at all", and I threw him out of the house.

What's Your Interpretation?

January 07

As I drove up to a house coming from Down-South, a house in St. Alban, Queens, New York; where a lady named Mrs. Bergist; to which my parent and other people where there. Either during that day or few days after, I had done something real terrible. As I got up in the morning and sat at a small round table, my mother sat across from me, and a family member to the right of her. She begins to ask questions about why and what I had done to my brothers. Why I did what I did and to have so much anger to throw his right leg out in the middle of the road.

As I finish my breakfast, I look past my mother out the window at the condition of the weather—to which it was a beautiful sunny day. Then for some reason I look back at her and said, "Yes, I did it . . . It was for his own good", then she replied, "His own good! Kill him". Then I stated, with some water filling up in my eyes—"It needed to be done", with no passion in my voice. As (my mother) she got up from the table. I begin to realize that I may be taped; I quickly got up, pack some clothes and place them in the backseat of a two door coupe-Mercedes-Benz, and heard the siren of the police.

I quickly ducked down and craw to the yard—left side of the house and snuck through the open fence into the neighbor yard, through the back, out onto the other side of the street. As I reach the second block a man and a woman (both white) came from behind and said, Excuse me sir . . . are you Mr. Bartley". Afraid to say no or to state my real name; I agree due to the fact that the couple look like undercover cops. So the man stated, "If so, you have stolen my father identity. He's near ninety (90) years of age, and how can he have a debt of over thirty-thousand dollars ($30,000)?" So then the woman phone for the police; I then slip into a house out the back, hide behind two cars, till I made it to a very busy house, that home a lot of kids. So I went in and there were another door to enter into the house, but a screen door with at least three (3) to four (4) huge dogs (at least three feet in height) waiting at the screen door. Without even—thinking of being attacks by the dogs. I open the screen door and stoop down for them to get a good sniff and begin to rub and pat them, as I make my way in, downstairs in the huge basement. The other kids coming upstairs, around out of their rooms; they must have known that the cops, even the FBI was looking for someone. So a young kid shows me where to hide for now. While making my way downstairs, one of the detectives came in the house questioning my whereabouts. Seem like the oldest kid act like he didn't see anyone or me pass by. While I was making my way around downstairs and as I was passing the stairway, I could see the detectives; as I hid behind one of the Pit Bulls that were along the stairs. I would rub one, then the other as I make my way to hidden wall behind the boiler. As soon as the kid close the door and told me to sit tight; the FBI appear outside of the house, trying to look through the basement window to see if I were there.

After they had search the premise, the kid came and told me that the coast is clear, but there were a few that haven't left yet. So as I make my way upstairs, the other kid open a compartment door to the right of me and stated, "They in the backyard", and for me to hide in the clandestine (shoot). As I begin to climb in, there were nothing for me to stand on, as I look down in the shaft-like wall—it look like one of those laundry-shoot, but fill with plastic hangers. I climb in but couldn't lift my left leg. As the detective re-question the kids in the yard and at the door; the kid that were helping me, helped lift my leg just in case if the detective peek in. Then down at the bottom of the step, the other kid pointed toward the basement window to alert us of the FBI and police searching at the side of the house, trying to look through the window. After they had left, I thank them for their assistance and left throughout the backdoor.

What's Your Interpretation?

_____

_____

_____

_____

_____

_____

_____

_____

_____

_____

_____

_____

_____

_____

_____

_____

_____

_____

_____

JANUARY 11

In a mall, running and hiding from something, and there were others hiding as well. So as I dip behind a clothes rack, I step out of the store and saw nothing but space—stars and planets. So I look up and said, "Your son needs you". As I went back into the store, I could see most of my friends running toward and passing me, so I turn and ran as well. Then all of a sudden large groups of bronze-wing like angels, whose face were like a shield helmet, came and scope my friends and took to the air; one came and grabs me up and told me to hold on. As soon as the huge bronze, full body plated-wing like angels scope me up; many guns shot, ring across the air, as bullets bounce of the wing of the bronze angel. As the angel cover me within it's wings, it took a big jump, yet fast but smooth as we head up toward the heavens; as those who were not grab by the angels, as most didn't made it, as I look back. As soon as we reach some strange planet, somewhat like earth; the giant huge bronze angel said to me, "You hold great power". What was so strange at the moment, when we left the other planet, it looked more like some giant spaceship, with an open sky roof; somewhat like a stadium.

So here I am in another world and leaving out from the school; the place is very familiar (In New York City near the Pier or I should say the Hudson River); yet this college were almost half of the city. As I left out down the block of stairs, toward a huge medical facility; I hop unto a bus, which looks like the old green line buses from the sixty (60's). As I step on with the book bag on my right shoulder, there I see three (3) of my friends talking among each other. One of them asks me where I was heading and I stated, 'to pick up my car that were borrow earlier'. As the bus approach the next stopping point, we ring the bell and order the driver to drop us off here. So we hop out like soldiers jump down from a helicopter. The area to me looks much like Jamaica Avenue in Queens, New York. As we approach an area, walk through a bus terminal garage and there my car—Black, but the two (2) back tires look like they had been chew or something took a couple of bite out of them. I look at the car and begin to walk around it, but seem worried. The guys and two (2) females said, "We need to get back and in before time. I stated to them, "Go ahead, and I will catch up with you later". As they left, I went inside the driver side and grab something out from underneath the consol; but didn't look what I have grab and immediately place it in my bag. I look at my watch which had no face or arm to tell me the time, but for some reason I knew I have to leave now before the second sun set. I begin to jog, keeping up pace and controlling my breathing, knowing that I had a long run back to the University near the Pier.

What's Your Interpretation?

JANUARY 18

In a gym-setting where many young men standing around waiting for someone to come; I begin to stated to the group, "Let play!" and the refs saying, "Black's Ball"; just before we begin, a white town car limousine pulls up into the gym unto the floor. A black bodyguard or driver got out and call to one of the tall guys that the boss needed to speak to him. The tall guy looked worried and stated, "I could him by the door"; me standing facing the tall man, decided to step into the limo, with my right leg outside of the limo. There sit an old slim pimp-like with long grey coat with a dark fur collar—like the coat needed to be clean. As I sat looking at him with a small smile or smirk and one (1) eye focus on the door. The slim guy said, "I am the last pimp to be known and since the guy didn't want to come in, I now pass my power unto you". So I thank him, step out and as he step out as well (looked more like Jim Brown—the football player), then the game begin, one of the guy on my team took a shot and went over pass the rim, I caught it as it came down and took it back out, dibble to the top of the key, drove to the basket, took off just before the line and dunk it with such authority; the crowd seem like they were waiting for the game to begin, as the other team missed the shot, I, coming down the side by the three (3) point line, one of the guy drive toward the basket, dish (pass) the ball to me as he draw in the defender, took the shot—the ball went clear into the net and the crowd went crazy.

Then I headed outside as someone took my place on the court. As I was telling a joke to a few folks, I turn to my car (black—Infiniti), a car was about to pull out into the road, then backup and had backed up to the trunk of my vehicle; scratching the keyboard that was or seem like painted on the edge of the trunk. As the car were about to pull off; I slap on the back and the back driver-side of the vehicle. The female stop and her and the male passenger look back and backed the car to park. They got out and before saying anything to the female, the male acted like I did something wrong; as I said to him, "Take one more step and you will feel the rapture". As he looks in my eyes, seeing the fear on his face, he steps back and away. So the female apology and we walk over to a picnic table, where she gave me her boyfriend's insurance card. We begin to talk—she stood about five feet-four inches, petite, dark skin but beautiful. I begin to ask her out on a date. She pulls out a piece of paper and gave or wrote down her number. In return I pull out my wallet and got my business card out to give to her.

What's Your Interpretation?

JANUARY 21

Just got finish taking a test, which seem like the final; so I got up and head in toward the living room, but it had two (2) beds. One near the kitchen open and the other near the opening toward the front door. I had a small round glass and pour myself a glass of bourbon. As I was taking a sip; a group of three (3), one (1) male and two (2) females came in. I quickly bend the top of the glass closed and place it under the bed. Then a guy named NDale asks, 'What are you hiding", as I reach further under the bed, pull out a VHS tape and said, "Put it in the VCR". As he insert the tape, one of the female slip under the cover with her back to me. As I grew and penetrate myself into her, the movie begins to play. As I got up stated, "I'll be back to retrieve the tape later". It was night time, as I head across the street, toward a house where the sun begins to shine.

As I stood in between the doorway of the living room and kitchen; in which the kitchen were full of people. To my left were two (2) boys, directly in front were an elderly woman, just behind her to her left were a middle-age woman and at the head of the table to the left of the elder, were a woman and in between them were a child in a car seat on the corner of the table. While the mother at the head of the table seem to change the baby, the baby begin to cry and kept swapping at the mother, as she begin to swing back at the baby; she then grab the car seat that the baby was in and tried to throw it across the room,; but the elder grab the car seat with the baby in it and the young woman behind the elder step in between the baby and the mother, and told the mother to relax. The mother begin to curse the baby stated, "The baby . . . gonna swing at me!" So as the mother sat back at the table and they slide the baby in the car seat back to the mother, as soon as she begin to change the pamper, the baby begin to

18

car and swing at the mother, making it difficult for the mother. Then she slings the baby over onto the floor by the door, where I stood. She got out of her seat and begins slapping at the baby. I wanted to stop her, but knowing with my involvement will cause uproar. As someone step in and pull the child from underneath, I walk away. As I step away, the mother yell at me saying, "Why you didn't step in and stop me?" There I knew trouble were about to begin as others look and approach me. So I left the house.

What's Your Interpretation?

JANUARY 29

s heading toward a huge hotel-like building with many store within. In the center inside were yellow golden color marble floors, as the light hit; brighten the atmosphere throughout the entire building. As I turn to my right and enter through a tall dark brown with black accent, as I enter, there I saw a man, whom seem to be promoting or of someone important; wearing a dark political type suit; sitting next to him on his right facing the audience were my pastor. Yet the room was small, sort of like one of those libraries with wood accent all around. There were a few church members as well, a total of no more than seven (7), including myself. As I stood and sat to the right of the pastor, to which it seem like the gentleman were announcing of running for office (not sure if it were for Mayor, Congress or Senate), but as he finish talking; the pastor stated, "We have a special guest", as most look on; "He has a book out and we need to show support". So the pastor announces me in and some of the church members begin to walk out. Yet, I felt like something heavy lifted off my shoulder. There were Ms. A, Deacons, the pastor's wife and a few ushers who stay to support, Yet Ms. H'well, looked upset; while others left like I own them something. As the pastor slide the book to the man. He stated to me, "I would like for you to be my running mate", because he heard of me in the past of helping other politicians, that I helped successfully to win, I agree and step out of the chamber like room.

As I was walking through the tall bushes along the highway, toward the south; there were two (2) white men behind me in a distant like they were hunting for something or someone. The man in front had on a black rubber iron type glove, as well as the man that were behind; with a pole and on the end of the pole where a camera or some sort of telescope. As I begin to walk fast, the two (2) men begin to step in a jogging motion. As they got closer, the man with the pole stated, "Go ahead and grab him". Within approximate ten (10) to twelve (12) feet as the man reach out to grab me, I ran and jump, then begin to fly into the air as my wings expand. As I flew over the cars and trucks, heading north in the middle of the highway, the man extended the pole to see the direction I was heading. As I step down into the forest-like medium between the two (2) highways, trying to lure them, thinking that I was heading back north or either hiding out. As I cross over to the other side in between the on-coming vehicles and slip into the wooded area to head back toward the south. The man with the pole were still searching, but the other man somehow were able to track me; as he alert the other man by walkie-talkie or cellphone; I flew up again and as the man swing the pole to tried to knock me down from the sky, I grab the end of the pole, and rip off the telescope. The other man went to assist his partner. I pull them both up from the ground as they hung unto each other on the pole, then I send a great shock down the pole and there they fell to the hard pavement on the highway.

What's Your Interpretation?

_____

_____

_____

_____

_____

_____

_____

_____

_____

_____

_____

_____

_____

_____

_____

_____

_____

_____

_____

_____

FEBRUARY 06

It was the day to pick up my brother and his wife from the station. Instead of using my car, I used a four (4) door (red—unsure if it were a Chrysler or Ford), but it had power. As I got there, he was the only one (1) waiting. As I set his bag [to which it were only one (1)], I ask, "Where your wife?" He kept silent, so I drove where I had left my car.

As we approach the vehicle, it were broken into, I open the trunk and saw papers scatter; look in the front seat, the glove department open, and papers all over but nothing really stolen. I took my key and insert in the ignition and notice feces were all over the ignition, as I pull the key out there were about four (4) Latinos guys coming around the corner, laughing and stated, "We're here in the neighborhood!" One (1) of them came up behind and grab me around the neck, as I prepare to defend the other three (3) and took the key in my right hand that had feces on it and stab the man in the eye. As I done that, my brother took out his weapon and begins firing at the men, hitting one (1), and I took out my weapon, shot and kill the man that had me in a choke hold and stated, "HE still rule!"

After the incident, we drove to the house and as we pull up, I ask my brother who have not spoken a word since I pick him up from the station. So I ask, "Where is she . . . why she wasn't at the station?" With the empty look he begin to withdraw his weapon, I turn from the kitchen into the living room behind the beam wall and headed downstairs in the basement, through a hidden door that no one knows about but me. As my brother lure around in the basement, as I slip upstairs and look downstairs at my brother, assuming that maybe he had killed her, but then there were a group of people trying to invade the house. So I pull out some heavy artillery as my brother did the same; then some of those that were already in the house upstairs covering all side and came downstairs to help assist my brother and me, as we clear the demons that surrounded the house.

What's Your Interpretation?

FEBRUARY 15

Being in a classroom, look like we just got finish studying or taking a test; to which I and a few got up and step out of the classroom. I took a left down the hall, then a right in to another room. I nodded my head toward the class and turn toward the stairs as others begin to get up and leave out of the classroom as well. I went down to the next level into what seem to be an apartment. I sat in the living room among the other men, that were there; as they communicate among each other. Then a woman came out, from the kitchen where the other women were, having their meeting of conversations. She stated something to me as I was watching a music gospel video on a black and color television (yes, a black and color television). As I agree to what was stated, I put on a light-weight iron like plated chest. Then one of the men begins to argue about me doing whatever I was supposed to do. With little fear, I stated, "Why don't you and your crews do it!" As my brother place his right hand against his chest and stated, "This is not the place", as my brother turn to me, "Go now, before it get dark"; So I got up and left out.

As I step out of the apartment building, which seem like I exit from a side door from the corner of the building, while at the same time, he comes out from the first door, which seem to be the main entrance to the building. As I back away, preparing to make a run, more of his crews begin exiting out of the building. There were many people along the sidewalk, but they soon disappear or less traffic; yet as I was about to cross the street, more and more cars were passing through. There were no corner or walkway to get to the other side, but to cross in-between the moving cars, there were four (4) lanes to cross just to get to the center. As I cross the first three lane, one of the crew cross into the fourth (4th) lane to cut me off, but one of the cars—push him pass me, down in a deep ditch. As I look back to my left, I sense a vehicle (look like a red ford mustang) heading toward me. So I quickly step into the fourth (4th) lane and within half a car length in distance, I step into the 'No Zone' center lane, as the car zoom behind me. As I turn and look back the other crews and him were making their way across the dangerous lanes. A young lady (dark smooth skin, low haircut, slim, dress in black outfit) pull up to me and told me to hop on. I got on the back of her scooter and we took off, losing the crews and him behind. I grab up to her breast and pull myself close behind her, to which she didn't reject my grasp. Then we pull over to a brown stone apartment which many young ladies were sitting among the steps; entering and exiting out the apartment. Then as we head toward up the five (5) steps, the traffic crease and the sidewalk became busy again.

What's Your Interpretation?

FEBRUARY 16

I just came in from outside, I assuming from school because I place my briefcase and books in the chair and place food that I purchase for myself on the table; it looked like a slice of pizza wrap with slice steak and salad—to which there were two (2) pieces. One (1) of my best friends, who is like a brother to me named Chris, came in and place his food on the table, sat and begin eating his food. I stated to him to not touch my plate, as I went over to get a drink. As I turn toward the fridge and got a bottle of coke; I turn back toward the table and notice my pizza sandwich were gone. I ask Chris, "Why would you do such a thing?"—He continues to eat my food. I try to let it go, but anger came over me and I took the weapon from my waist and pointed at him and demand some sort of funds. He refuses to repay and challenge me that I need to put the weapon away. So I aim at his right shoulder and shot at him. He turns and fell with a hole from his left shoulder; so someone heard the shot and came in stated, "the cop is coming!" So I place the gun in the lower part of my back and step out of the house. I turn right, down the driveway into the backyard, just before the cops pull up to the house. I look right, then left and across the neighbor backyard to ensure no one see me. So I jump the log fence in the neighbor's yard and heard a cop saying, "He's over here!" I quickly took three (3) quick step and flew into the air, trying to head in the opposite direction the cop's cars were facing, but the wind were pushing me backward. I tried to fly against the wind, but the harder I try, the lower I was getting to the ground. As I avoid the telephone's wires, I turn and went along with the wind and flew higher and farther into the next town.

As I landed at the school, went in through the side—rear entrance, through the locker room—thinking where I need to hide the gun. I thought about putting in one (1) of the lockers, as I cross the seat of a huge tracker or lawnmower; as one (10 of the black janitor see me cross over, due to [it] blocking the path toward the open door, knowing that I have to reach it before it close when the bell ring. See when the bell ring or if the police trap me; the jail is just to the left, up the stair where a steel door open. As I came across, I ask the other janitor, "Where's the way out?" and he stated, "right at the door . . . first door to the left" So with caution, I turn right and up the left as quickly as possible, which took me to the lobby of an upscale mall-like arena. I saw the elevator to the right about one (1) o'clock right of me. So I decide to take the stair outside to the roof, to which I flew, barely stepping on the loose sliding unto the roof-top balcony. There were a lot of people on the roof-top as well as on the other side of the building across from me. It was pack, people looking and hanging out the window, like a parade where going by. Then a scream from the crowd as one of the police officer were falling as the other officer try to grab his hand, but no luck; to which I were surrounded by police officers, but they didn't recognize me. To my right were a glass or window where everyone one were looking at the actions. There were a white detective and there were a slot between the wall and the window pane (a good spot to place the weapon and disappear) that way if I do get caught, they won't have any evidence. As I turn to the left, [they] begin to scream again, as another man leap toward death. In order to stop the madness which gave me an idea, were to place the gun between the wall and glass window and jump in flight, but the detective kept looking over at me, every time I move my right hand to sneak the weapon in place. So I waited for the next scream and everyone look to see who had jump or fell to their death. I place the weapon and the detective saw and realizes who I was, begin banging on the glass. I turn left, passing the officers and ran to the edge as they tried to grab me and took a leap and my wings open up and I took flight as everyone look in fear.

What's Your Interpretation?

_____

_____

_____

_____

_____

_____

_____

_____

_____

_____

_____

_____

_____

_____

_____

_____

_____

_____

_____

_____

_____

February 21

At a small house, getting prepare to get a car, but really wanted to just get out and hang with a few people. Yet, He wanted to come along with my brother and me; not to be around, but to lure me into darkness to destroy me. So we three (3) got in the car and begin to drive off. As we join with the other cars on the freeway, the only way to escape is to destroy him in some way. There a hill, as we climb, I floor the pedal to the floor, preparing to jump the car. As we came over the hill, I turn the car to the left as we begin to fly up and flew over several cars toward our death. I told God within me for my brother sake—'Forgive me, sorry my brother' as we came crashing down toward the roadway. A loud explosion as we three (3) hit and flew toward the freeway's wall, just before He tried to grab the steering wheel. The car evaporates in pieces, as we three grasp unto the wall. The walls were wood beam-like with ash tray, flowers made out of glass and those wall climbers. I could see my brother to the left, above me approximate four (4) feet apart, as I carefully grab the "wall-climbers", as I lower myself toward the ground. As He tried to reach me to make me loose balance to fall to my death, I reach over to the left and almost grab the ashtray, then grab over to the right and re-grab the wall-climber; while in the process of losing my grip, I push myself away to the right and back dive into a lake as the other two (2) follow me in.

As I came up, I swam over to the other bank and there were camera crews, with the director stating, "Cut!" It was like we were in the basement of a house fill with water. The camera crews wanted to go through a pike-like hole (which had very little room), I know if I go into this or through this pike and get struck, I had no way to turn around within the pike. As I stay hidden out of reach from Him, trying to stay underwater (yet breathing like a fish) for a long period of time. I saw my brother swim deep down under a mirror-like wall. I went up for air and back down passing the camera crews to lure away from Him. As I swam underneath the mirror wall and up on the other side, there were a hill with a trail on the side to my left and podium, stone with grass and vine has grew, like the place has been vacant for hundred of years. There was a sidewalk along the path of the bank which was on my right. The weather was mild, warm. The wind was calm, yet comfortable. As I swim to my left, there a young woman and my brother saying, "Follow me"; as we head toward a house sitting among the field. As we approach closer, we see Him coming out, so we then turn around and begin jogging in the other direction along the trail at the side of the hill. As we were moving along side the bank, I look up and see Him and two (2) other men in a jeep, passing above along the dirt road. We stop and then tried to climb the vertical grassy wall. As I were slipping in the process of falling unto the ground, I push myself away from the grassy wall, down into the water; as my brother and the young lady follow behind; as we swim underwater to the other side. As we came up on the other side of the bank, we were in the middle of the mall, which seem to be deserted for many years with grass that had grew between the marble slate, vines along the walls and poles. As I look at the dark night through the broken glasses.

What's Your Interpretation?

March 05—
Forward Push

Walking with a gentleman, to which seem like a parole officer in street clothing, as well as myself; but I'm more like an attorney heading toward house to visited a man, who seem to be on house arrest or to check up on him on his status with the job and being at home at a certain time; a formal convict, who seem to be under stress from work and requesting a different job. He—the formal convict stated that he minding his own business, working hard and still getting pick on for no reason; yet in fact, trying to get prepare for court hearing. As we sat and finish talking, went over to a friend's home who had a female that seem as if we dislike each other or some sort of secret that she were going to make public, I got up and left out. As I see the young lady left out and enter into another house, as I enter through the side door. Then stated to her, "leave my house!"; as she approach in a violent manner, I did some sort of martial art move, which I push her up toward a wall; in which she hit with such a force, that she nip an object on my right knuckle-pointer finger. I pick her up and before leaving out of the house, check up and down the street to ensure no one was around, as well as checking windows to make sure no one was looking out. I went two (2) houses down to the back door and lay her body in the living room and slip back out back through the yard, back in my house, in through the side door, back over to the formal convict; to which there were a few cops at the door. The formal convict or suspect stated that a young lady were found dead in a house; so as the suspect's attorney, I excuse him from answering any other questions of who may had murder the young lady. As we sat and talk how we are going to handle the case, we walk into the chamber or court room; to which the suspect sitting in the witness seat, being question by the defender, who named was Regina, from the South Central drama show. As my client repeatedly stated 'he knows nothing of the matter'; there was a step ladder being used as an exhibit. I reject what was being stated and grab the step ladder and toss it backward to the back of the court room. Then men in a tan suit came in through the door with a white shirt with blood on it and took a cotton swap and wipe the step ladder with the blood on it; which I cut my finger on it during the toss. The tan suited detective then stated, "I got the evident and it's his blood"; as he pointed to me.

What's Your Interpretation?

MARCH 09

Sitting in the classroom as the professor talks about the U.S. Economy, then one of the student; a Caucasian want to try to show how smart he knows about the subject and challenge the professor of what he think is best. Where as many of the student, as well as myself, tend to ignore of what he had to say. As I turn away and look further throughout the book; as the professor corrected the young man, I turn and stated my known information to which everyone and the professor agree. This ended the class session, so I place the textbook in my briefcase and left out without looking back. As I step out in the hall turning left up the stair, to which many worshippers were entering to and from inside the church. The greeters were standing at the entrance, greeting and handing out programs to incomers. As I took one of the program and enter, there on the stage were various singers, practicing a few songs; as the controllers in the back adjusting the lights and sounds. I walk toward the front and sat at the second row from the center left, but I knew that I usually sit in the fourth row from the front, next to the young lady. Since service doesn't start in the next twenty to thirty (20-30) minutes, I decided to step outside till it time for the service to begin. So I walk to the back, out in the waiting area, turn to my right and decided to step outside the front of the church. Many folks were standing around screaming. As I look across the highway, I see people line up along the wall as cars speed by. Then two (2) ladies ran out after one of the vehicle speed pass almost being tap by a box truck, as the vehicles blow their horn and I can hear the two (2) ladies said, "Ok, let's go"; as they pass across the line to get to the sidewalk. I look to my right and see that the vehicles are coming down from the bridge (which looks more like the Verrenzro Bridge in New York) in great speed. Looking down to my left as everyone were moving up the line—getting ready to take their chances to cross the highway, in their Sunday best. I ask myself why they just don't cross at the light, but notice there were no street light for miles and unable to park in the church's parking lot, because it were full. Then I ask God, 'are they willing to die to come to church to hear the message or to worship you?' As one of the old ladies with a middle age kid about to cross over; an Nissan Dotson came across the line and stop in front of them, facing on-coming traffic, stated something in Spanish accent, 'Why don't they just build a bridge, so y'all don't get hit out here in the street'; as they scream the wheel and pull off before a silver Chrystal come roaring down as the three (3) step out. The silver Chrystal turn with such a force to the left to avoid hitting the people, that it spin in the other lane going in opposite direction backward as the driver in the vehicle reverse the wheel and then shift back into drive to keep control of the car; spin the vehicle to the left back into the other lane before the other cars came. As I turn looking toward along the rail, there's two (2) elderly ladies crossing with no help and a car came and hit both, sending one twenty (20) feet in the air and the other knock down. As both laid along the sidewalk, I ran down toward the ambulance to assist, as I look at one (1) of the elder lady, circling around them. The EMS (emergency medical service) took of the lady on the gurney to place in the back of the ambulance, while the other elder woman laid lifeless, blood and plasma—yellowish blot as the flies buzz by the lifeless body. The EMS stated, "Don't touch her, she could be affected!", but something told me to reach down and touch her. Then I felt something strange as there were some sorts of danger if I did. Yet, regardless of the situation, I reach down and place my hand upon the lifeless body's forehead and a light shine behind me and the elderly lady woke up.

What's Your Interpretation?

_____

_____

_____

_____

_____

_____

_____

_____

_____

_____

_____

_____

_____

_____

_____

_____

_____

_____

_____

_____

_____

MARCH 18

Come on baby sing song—and we gonna listen all night long
Right on baby listens to me—This how we learn the ABC
It truth—it's permission by Ludacris

Walking in an arena seeing wrestlers talking to the audience, then a wrestler came toward the ring as he beat up and toss one man out the ring; then I get in and toss the guy who came into the ring as well as the other wrestlers. As the crowd begin to cheer and boos; more wrestlers came from the back and begin to fight among each other as two (2) of the ladies' wrestlers came into the ring. One (1) of the wrestler (bad) grab one of the lady and toss her upon his shoulder as the other wrestler toss the other lady (good) over the rope, into another wrestler; as I stood and sat in a chair outside of the ring. More and more wrestlers (good) came out to clear the ring. Then a black wrestler who caught the lady, that were toss out of the ring; I went over and told him, "go ahead and clear the ring"; while I grab hold to carry the lady in my arm. While he went in toward the ring, I took the lady and we sat in a black leather cushion chair. As the black wrestler clear the ring, another wrestler came out but white—same height, wore same outfit [overall with dark shade, clean shave head] cheering on his brother.

After the scene was over, I walk down the aisle leaving the arena and enter into the living room of an apartment. Noticing that I was alone; I went in near the kitchen to turn on the lamp which light up like the nightlight that you plug into the wall. As I turn to go to bed and went to sleep, leaving the light on for my parent and my brother—if they were to come late. Then I heard a noise, woke up but still laying, open my left eye and saw a shadow standing near to me. Unable to open my right eye, due to laying on my right side, trying to push myself up; but the shadow kept holding me down. Then I push myself up, still unable to see from my right eye, as I look for the shadow with my left; but were only able to see my long bridge of my nose in front of me, like I were looking through a tunnel. As I slowly peek around the corner toward the hallway into the living room, I begin to search for the switch to turn on the lamp and notice as I was able to see with both eyes. There were a light in the kitchen, as I slowly approach the kitchen, there my mother sitting at the glass table—I had bought for her in 1989; as my brother were fixing her a late night snack, hearing her said: "Your father will be home soon".

As I enter back toward the living room, there were camera around shooting a music video title; 'It's Truth—It's Permission', and Ludacris were the director for one of the three (3) boys—group artist. After the song they added a bonus and I came in as a surprise guest and begin rapping and singing; "Come on baby sing songs—and we're gonna listen all night long, Come on baby listen to me—this is how we learn the ABC".

What's Your Interpretation?

_____

_____

_____

_____

_____

_____

_____

_____

_____

_____

_____

_____

_____

_____

_____

_____

_____

_____

_____

_____

_____

_____

MARCH 20

Laying or sleeping on the sofa, heard a sound within my home; I lift my head up and peek toward the door, to which doesn't seem like anyone were there and no light from the doorway. So I closed my eyes and rest my head back unto the pillow; then once again second later, I heard the door open. I this time jump up and dash to the door; this time it were slightly open. Just as I open the door, there a woman in her mid to late eighty (80's), standing with a few items of clothing in her arm. I ask, "Can I help you?", as I look down at her. She stated, "Yes, we're moving into our new apartment", and I stated, "There must be a mistake?—because I'd still live here". As we step into another apartment that were open, the elderly lady sat in one of those basket couch, but then I notice that her face were round, tan smooth but crack—like a crocodile's skin. As there were many other middle-age women, about three (3) of them; discussing in frustration of the mistake that the apartment manager made toward, according to the set-up or arrangement for their move-in and the apartment they should be in. As I turn back toward the door of my apartment, two (2) men bringing in clothes, so I head into my apartment and stated to them, "You gonna have to take those out of here and place them in the other apartment". As the two (2) men stand looking at me, like they own the apartment, I quickly grab a knife and with demand as I'm ready to offend my position; they backed out and went into the other apartment. So I went into the bedroom and there were a few boxes and clothes that didn't belong to me, so I grab two (2) boxes to take over to the other apartment.

As the three (3) women continue arguing on the situation of the apartment; in return I stated in a forceful voice, "How can y'all move into an apartment that is still occupied and didn't y'all see me sleeping on the sofa?—Idiots!" and turn around to retrieve the rest of their items. As I enter back into the bedroom, the apartment manager enter into the other apartment to make amend with the folks in the other apartment as the three (3) women continually still trying to out talk each other on complaining about the situation. As I enter into my bedroom, another dude or black guy were laying on top of my bed, being tired from hauling furniture and clothes in the apartment. I violently told him to get out, as I grab an arm of coats; as he grab a few black bags and stated, "I'm from the South and we live above the ground, and you wouldn't say it in my face to move out". As I walk behind him, I told him, "Then turn around and I tell it up in your face . . . I'm from New York and where I'm from, I live above the streets, you Pussy!" as I threw the coats at him and his woman following behind.

What's Your Interpretation?

MARCH 21

Walking through a chamber to which the pastor (Ron) standing and preaching behind the podium, about piercing and marks. I move to the front row to which there were fold-up chair in this small sanctuary. After preaching the congregation left, only the other pastors, ministers as well as I stay for the meeting. Pastor (Ron) stated, "If you wish to preach, you have to remove your earring. It who you represent, because the people need a leader" By hearing this I know he were talking about me; so as the meeting were over, the pastor and myself left out to the side, while the others talk among themselves; and the pastor stated to me before I approach the stairway, "We are waiting for you to take over. You are a great speaker and you don't even know what is in store for you. Be the leader God expecting for you to be". So I went upstairs entering through the door of an apartment into the kitchen, which was very small only five (5) maximum of people may be able to fit in this kitchen. The kitchen were somewhat old fashion, white gas stove, ice box, thirteen (13) inch white-color T.V., one (1) window with apple-pear type curtains. There were at least five to seven (5-7) people in this small kitchen including myself. A dark heavy-set woman came in and sat in the seat with her back facing near the opening to the living room. Knowing I was not in likeness on this woman, but she lean over to kiss me on my chest ask me, "how's your day went?"—In respond I stated, "relaxing", as other chat and watch this small white-color T.V. I lean over to her and kiss her on her stomach and grab the back of her head with my right hand and gave a tongue kiss. Second later I could feel my bowel move as dropping of stain were on the pillow. I grab the pillow and stated, "I'll be back"; as I race through the hanging beads through the mountains of clothes, turn left through the hanging clothes and look to the first (1st) door on the right to which it were a closet of clothing and scarfs. The door to the left were the restroom, as I rush in pulling my pant down, grabbing my rear with my right hand as I tried to hold some back; but still it were no stopping it and finally sat down to relieve the boiling heat from my stomach.

What's Your Interpretation?

_____

_____

_____

_____

_____

_____

_____

_____

_____

_____

_____

_____

_____

_____

_____

_____

_____

_____

_____

MARCH 28

Leaving from the bedroom after using the computer, heading outside of a two (2) story brownstone like building; cross the street down three (3) or four (4) houses to the right and saw a young girl struggling with some bags. So I offer my assistance to help with the bags as she agrees. As we approach the front door, I place the bag just inside the door not entering in the house. I turn around after being thank, to head across the street to go to the store. Military like cops with NYMD logo's patch on the upper left of their chest and on their baseball caps, with dark blue pants, black strip line down on the left side and military like boots; came and rush up to me order for me to get down on the ground. As I lay in the middle of the street, as they place the cuff around my wrist. They pick me up off the clean tar mat ground; which were glitter with small diamond—rubies like pebble stones and walk me over to the brown stone building. They un-cuff me as they stated to my parent, "He may have to serve fifteen-years (15) and need to be at the court to face the judge in a few hours". I begin to think if I'll be able to live in a building for fifteen-years (15)? So I and a few families members head over to a building that seem to be a catholic church; as I walk in the side door, there were a lady judge. The courtroom was pack with white men and ladies entering and exiting through the door with files and papers in hand. There sitting on the side were jury and in the stand were one (1) of my friend named Eric, who also were arrested for helping. As he explain; there a television that show the event, as he stated what and why as the scene grow as if we were all there looking far across the street. As he explained, "There were an accident and I ran to grab up the two (2) kids—both females and move from the sidewalk as one (1) of the car fell from the sky and standing in front of the wooded beam light pole. A few parts fell toward our way as we dip left and right; then in time move from in front of the pole before the truck crashed into it". After listen to the story, the jury verdict were guilty and for him to serve up to seven (7) years; as the officers lured us through the backdoor into the prison. There seeing some of my friends and a priest; as they look at a big screen T.V., then I begin to write down how we can change the law and planning of escaping.

What's Your Interpretation?

# APRIL 01

Sitting in class as the professor wrap up the lesson for the
day and giving his input on politic. As he finish debating
the wrongness, and what the government should do; I lash
out in a jokey but serious statement, "Then why don't you run for
office?" As most of the students giggle and others looked in shock.
As the professor look at me with a stare, I then said, "You not going
to fail me, because I have a different opinion—are you?", as we pack
our belonging; I headed on home. As entering, I notice I was in jean
and a T-shirt (which is shocking!), but few minutes ago, I was in my
grey suit, white shirt with matching grey tie with black specks on
them. As I lay in the living room floor watching T.V. and testing out
my new phone (that I've invented) got a call from my best friend,
while at the same time my mother came in and ask how my day was.
As I respond back that it went O.K., my friend was coming through
the door passing the bedroom down the hall to where I was. As we
sat on the floor and he discussing about what went on his job and
how his car seem to need some work or to be look at, I turn seeing
my mother putting up new curtains and looking out the window,
waiting for my father to come home; as the sun glare into my eyes.
I know that my friend wanted me to go hangout with him, but tried
to give him a hint that maybe next time or had some things to do
later on, as I show him my phone. So he got up as we shook hand,
saying to my mother, "good bye mom", as we always call each other
mother—'mom'; cause we know each other for many years. As he left
out through the door, I put on my sneaker and told my mother, "I'll
be back, need to check on a few things"; then she stated, "Be home
soon, before your father comes in the next hour"

As I step out and lean against a wooded fence that you see on a farm. A cat (tan hair) past from underneath me as I watch the cat go unto the grass in the opening. There was another cat further away meowing. I stand watching thinking that it was a mating call, to which I never saw cats mating. So I stand watching, but notice the tan-hair cat in the grass, stood up on it two (2) hind legs and in a squatting position with it right paw, pulling up it hairs from it rear end lifting it right leg in a football stance and beginning to pee; as if it didn't want any to get on it hairs; to which it were like the cat were pulling up its dress. As the cat finish it came toward me, as I begin to walk away from it; because I didn't want it to rub up against me, leaving the terrible scent.

As I turn around a small car heading in my direction almost pinning me near another car and a pole; as the man tried to stop his vehicle but his car kept sliding. The man had two (2) bulls in his vehicle as he tried to get them back behind the wooded fence. As he kept sliding by coming to a halt, the two (2) bulls got out; as I avoid one (1) of the bull which seem to be very aggressive. As the man got out and lure the female in through the gate. I stood over by the opening as the male came charging toward me and with a leap over the bull; the bull fell face forward to the left up against the wall; as the owner took hold of the bull and pushed the bull into the gate. Yet it was strange to see a bull in the back seat and the male bull in the front seat. As the owner and I laugh at the situation of getting control of the bulls, another owner leading a purple horse with S-curl-like hair style. As the horse enter in through the door, it turn it head and wink at me with it long eyelashes and blew a kiss. As the bull's owner look at me, I turn saying, "I get'em all, even animals loves me", as I laugh turning away as the lady behind the counter look at me as if she were offended by my remarks.

What's Your Interpretation?

APRIL 08

Unsure if I were in a classroom setting or a room in a basement as three (3) of my friends and a gentleman who look somewhat like Gregory Park; planning to sneak into a bank without any evidence of break-in, which would be done early after work. So we went through a tunnel, open a door that lead right where all the money was place in a tin-like box. He handed each of us, two (2) army green like bags to start filling the bags with nothing but money. After filling up the bags, he said, "I will meet y'all over at point 'B'"; which is at the building that he live in, where there not much known trouble, but have to avoid the slims.

As we loaded, the known 'formal drug-lord' now educator's vehicle and mine, we four (4) drove off and ensure no one (1) where following us as we turn various street, before we park the cars at an assign location. We got out of the vehicle, with our stacked bags over our shoulders and saw a few dogs lunge out from the building, as we walk a half of block as the dogs slowly but increasing their steps. We slip into a store that seems to once have been a barbershop. There a woman, who seem to be waiting for us, as we slip through the abandon shop passing through another door into the back of the store. As she took the bag and place it on or in a scale elevator tube, the smallest of my friend stated, "Quiet . . . the dogs out in the front". As one (1) of the larger dog pushed their way through the front boarded up door; just enough to squeeze through. We stand behind the door and wall to keep out of site, as they sniff behind seats and counters. A small hound (brown and white coat) came out from the side through a hole in the wall and grabs hold of my right hand or palm near the pinky finger. As I lift the dog and shook it off, the other two (2) large dogs took notice and came charging at the dog, as my friend held the door. The woman stated, "Put something up against the door quick, before they notice the other opening on the side". So the woman slip into the tube-elevator and stated to us to be sure we be at out point of destination. As I force the little dog back through the hole, the other dogs notice and I stated to my friends, "As soon as they enter the hole, dash out!" So one (1) went to the right side of the wall of us as the little dog squeeze back through the opening on the left, with the German Sheppard following behind. Then once again the little dog grabbing hold of my right palm as I look at it small row of canine teeth, as the dog growl. So as the two (2) dogs were half way through, we made our move, turning the door to lock it in place and place a few boxes at the hole that the dogs push through. I then shook of the little dog again behind the door as we four (4) step out of the store. There a wagon; wooded with red pulley or handle with rope tie to it. As the three (3) got in, I lift the rope that were tied to the red handle and begin pulling till we got to a black small vehicle. So they got out and we got into the car, as we can hear the police siren; in which the three (3) dogs were trackers for the police officers. So we quickly made a U-turn and drove down a few blocks, parking the vehicle a half a block away from our destination and enter into the building to the second floor. As we enter the gloomy hallway, knock on the only door that was on the second floor. The door open by the lady we met at the abandon store 'barbershop'; told us to come on in, as she smile. As we enter through into the living room, there the professor sitting on the leather sofa, as the other two (2) young lady counting countless of money through the counting machine as they mark, label and package the money across the six (6) table that were set in a round setting in the kitchen. As we eight (8) celebrate, as I held a glass of bourbon in my right hand and the formal bank robber said, "This is the greatest heist ever and there is a major shut down of every bank in the State and my career is done". As we continue to hear the siren, I then notice multiple cars parking rear first in a diagonal park. Many police or undercover police officers got out of nothing but detective-like vehicles. We were wondering how they would know we were here? I thought of escaping to the roof top, but no one was making a move. The money amongst the table was packed and ready to be delivered. I begin to think how long we all will be in prison—knowing it could be up to life. As I and my friends look toward the man, as he sit with masses tears flowing down from his eyes, as one (1) of the young ladies who were counting and packing the money, wiping the water among his cheeks. So I blot out, "We need to make a run for it . . . why sit and give up!?" As the officers came through the door, as I was about to dish into the room in the back; there were laughter and hugs, like a hug celebration. I didn't know what was going on, as party hats were being distributed out and others from the slum community entering. The leader stated, "It were a test to see if we were going to do the blame game or just leave one (1) behind, but you three (3) stayed; this were to paid the Mayor and some of the police staffs"; to which the mayor knows about this and is also getting a piece of the pie, actually everyone within the building is getting their share as they praise and respected us as the greatest ever. Then a kid came to me, around ten (10) or eleven (11) years of age; small curly afro, maybe East Indian complexion, ask if I had any spare clothing. As I place my arm around the young kid, I said, "Sure, come". As we leave the party. As the room light up and notice the money being handed out among the folks, the young girl that were sorting the money earlier call out to me and say she will have our money and will see me home tonight; to which she had a smooth beautiful Indian complexion. I assume she was my wife, because there was a matching ring on her and mine finger.

What's Your Interpretation?

APRIL 16

Coming out from a meeting from a school, church like building; heading through a subway like hall; as I headed up the stair to drop off a package. By going in the direction, I have to ensure no one follows me to the building or which was an apartment. As I pass a middle age black man; who stated to me, "Be careful"; as he speak into his left wrist, as he continue to sweep the hallway. Another man tried to approach me in a bully way, as I prepare to defend by any such movement. As he passes me asking, "What you got there? Where you're heading" As I turn to him stating, "Why you want to know, and are you looking to start something?" as he smile and enter the stairway. I waited to see if he were going to follow behind. As the sweeper stated to me, "It seem like he didn't want to mess with you" with a small laugh; as I begin to head down the hall along with the crowd. Coming out through the other stairway as the door open, he step out unto the hallway, assuming he were to follow me, but were caught by surprise that I haven't really move from the spot. As he follows the crowd out, I slip through an unauthorized door; up a few steps and out onto the sidewalk. As I approach a house into the room to hide the brown bag behind the cabinet in the wall. As I step out through the side door, a couple of dogs ran toward me from the backyard—barking as if they were going to attack me. As I brace for the attack, one (1) of my best friend came in through the gate, to meet his' dogs. I stated to him, "I'll be back for us to head out" He replied, "I'll be home"

I got into my car and head into a parking lot where two (2) ladies were cleaning out of their light blue Plymouth Chrysler. As I pull up next to the vehicle on the passenger side facing in opposite direction, I got out as the two (2) ladies walk away toward a mall lot building. I craw in the opening of the backdoor as I laid across the seat, feeling underneath the driver seat and the backseat; unsure what I was searching for but got up and got back into my car heading out the back-way through a dirt road, between trees.

As I was leaving out of the building, there she sitting near the door, down the sidewalk where one (1) of the neighbor from the attach building. As I were leaving, he walk pass me to talk to her. As I turn as he lean closer to her. So I begin to punch him to the side of his face, but it didn't seem to fade him. Then a hammer appear and I gave one (1) good swing, just before he kiss her and I grab around his neck with my left hand and swing him away as he fell back and ran. I then begin to go down the street back to the house to meet up with my friend, for us to check what was in the bag. As I open the gate the two (2) dogs came running toward me and the little dog as he approach, I drop down to the ground; as he brush me against my head; growling in a playful way.

What's Your Interpretation?

APRIL 23

While standing along with a group of people in a tube like hallway with fences along the side in a building, waiting for something or someone to come—ready in arms; in a subway like setting but no tracks. Standing and waiting in position as the light dangling above our heads. My brother and a few others went down below, closing the fence-door. Then down coming out from the tunnel were like zombies running with force along the fence, as we begin loading rounds into them, as I shout out, "Aim for head!", as my brother and the others held the gated fence door with large logs, as we on the ramp continue to jab through the opening with knives and taking aim as more and more pile in. Then they were coming from through the door on the second level where we were standing; so my brother and the others brace the logs up against the gated fence, as I command everyone to break out; as some made their way through the back and others up three (3) steps to the side door. I were looking for an alternate route, because they were moving too slow to get out. I look up to the ceiling thinking to crawl up into, because 'they' were getting close. As one (1) of 'them' touches one (1) of the man, he quickly shakes and became one (1) of 'them'. So as everyone got through the door, I then follow the two (2) other men up in the ceiling to head out the other way as I and the other men move on.

I enter into my apartment and sat on the sofa. As I was watching T.V. the light above the dining table caught my eye and notice it begin to shake, then I heard a saw and drill, like someone were sawing and drilling from above. As I stood up, the light fell onto the table and there's a hole from the neighbor above with a lot of commotions going on. I looked up at the hole as one (1) of the workers looked back and I stated, "Who gonna fix this!?" As the worker respond, "He will fix the problem", a young lady stated, "No need to worried about that, till my renovation is done" As the workers left from my sight and the young lady turning away. I jump up and pull myself through the hole, seeing many workers moving, placing and sawing; as they were pretty much renovating the whole apartment. As I look for the young lady, one (1) of the workers was going to place a toilet over the hole as they measure the length of the pike. I went over and remove the toilet with force and stated, "The hole will be replace with my lamp and no toilet will be place over my dinner table"; as the young lady came back in to disrupt the issue, with my demands and threats, "If this toilet is place in this spot, I will destroy you with great multitude", and as she went into the living room which used to be a kitchen stated, "who is you to tell me where I can place or do in my apartment?", as she called out for her boys. When they saw me, they went and left out of the apartment. One (1) of the worker order everyone to stop in order to begin working on the hole in the floor, as I drop back down through the hole; to open the door to let the worker in to replace the hole and the light fixtures.

JOHN EDWARD FARMER

What's Your Interpretation?

MAY 06-08

S tanding in the hallway, waiting as if I were about to be introduce to the media. As many line up against the wall, smile and talking among each other; as a few with papers in hand going to and from in the hallway. As I make my way down the hall, as the people clap, but then I notice two (2) men following up real close behind me, as I turn to face them, to challenge the problem. They stop as I back up through an opening door. As I headed down the hall where as the wall were filled with square whitish-greyish tiles, yet bright lights overhead. As I peek outside as if I were looking for someone; then I made a dash over the chain fence that was only two (2) foot off from the ground. Trying to make across the field and then hid behind a bush. Look to the right of the bush to ensure no one was following me. There I enter in a building with many folks were taken their seat; I then walk across handling out flyers to those passing by. I then got to the front of the crowd and begin to thank those for coming and begin to speak about various issues around or about the churches and the communities. After getting the audiences pump up; went and sat over at a desk and begin signing books as those approaches to get my signature. As more were coming in the lobby, I got up to head out the back when a woman approach—whom look someone like my past supervisors, stating, "Your schedule need to be change", In return I stated, "My schedule is set in stone" and left into a warehouse setting with nothing but black painted stairs. Some were escalator, yet spiral ladder type regular stairs all in this warehouse setting. As I were trying to make my way out, there were two (2) men who seem to be chasing me, as I down hop from stair case to stair case, trying to reach one (1) of the three (3) doors to get out. One (1) door to the rear of the building were on the second floor, the door to the left of the building were one (1) floor level up or about four (4) feet from the ground and the third which were to the front of the building down the stairs, as if going into the basement. As I tried to avoid the two (2) men, looking to get to the rear door, the man hop up preparing to capture me, but I jump up to the escalator, up looking for another way out, as I look out the large square four (4) panel window. As the other man coming from a different stair, I jump in between the rail on to the step, hop down to the front door and unloose the lock and turn the lock; then dash back up the stair, so that they won't see what I had done. As I tried to have the second man to be drew near, making them both think they had me trap. As I make them come closer to the rear of the building, I then quickly ran up to the 'cat-man walk' or rail, that you may see in a stadium or masses churches up near the roof; ran across to the other side down the escalator and onto the spiral stairs; hid behind a wall and waited as they looked for me. As soon as their backs were turn, I quickly ran out around the wall and just as I grab the door knob, one (1) of them yelled out, "There he is . . . grab him!" I open the door and there I was free.

What's Your Interpretation?

MAY 13

s walking through the gym, there I met up with a group of men and women standing among each other discussing issues on the finance's budget. As one of them pass a book that were larger than the standard eleven and a half (11 ½) by eight and a half (8 ½) across into another hand. As I took a glance at the cover, trying to read the title, which seem to read: How to Obtain Finance; I then turn and saw a female, as I watch as she approach a table; seemly to be inquiring information. I turn and took another look at the book, now being passed back to the men, titling: 'Manage Calculation in Money Making'. So I left from the group and head over to where the lady was and put my arm around her waist, as she push herself closer to me and we head into toward the hallway; as we see people entering in the elevator. But something told me if I got on the elevator a problem may occur. As passing the elevator—she said: "We not going to get on or are we going to wait for the next one (1)? I stated, "I think it's best to take the stairs"; as I check my weapon. So we head up the stairs to the next floor and as I open the door slowly, as we proceed down the narrow hallway, the elevator door open as the car seem to be stuck between floors. Something deep down stated that I got to get them out, before something very bad would happen. As I grab a rope or cable, which were on top of the elevator; tied it to a door handle and drop the other end through the opening of the elevator door-hatch. As the first two (2) got out, I look up as an elevator coming down on the other end. Its stop about four (4) floors above and just as the next to last person coming through the opening; the elevator above shift over slowly and above the elevator that the young lady and I were assistance those get out. Then the elevator begin to vibrate violently; just as we pull the lady onto the floor, I jump down on top of the elevator to pull the heavy man through; which I twist and turn the man side to side. As he was finally able to get through, I now have to quickly get him up onto the floor; as he struggling—pulling himself up along the wall. I got underneath to give him a lift, as the elevator beneath us slowly being to drop. As the others grab hold of the heavy man, pull him onto the floor. Just as I grab the cable, the elevator drop about two (2) feet and the elevator above—jerk up and begin to come down fast. I quickly pull myself up and onto the floor, just miss the bottom of my boot; as the elevator scream pass slamming on top of the elevator, as it crash to the deep dark bottomless floor; giving off a thundering sound.

I then ran to my car and we drove toward the beach, to which there were an old house that seem to be abandon, but it were a foreclosure house; I was working on to prepare as a vacation home. As I park the car, three (3) men and two (2) ladies were walking toward us; as she went to greet them. Two (2) of the men went to the trailer that were attach to their pickup (black huge F150) truck and back out the lawnmower, but having a hard time handling the lawnmower. I took hold of the steering wheel and back it up along the gravel rocks and sands, to the edge of the driveway to the right instead to the left, which had water on both side—like a island as I look at the house far left, didn't know I had back up this far; but didn't understand why I had this lawnmower, when there were no grass to cut.

What's Your Interpretation?

MAY 19

After leaving out from the place of Worship, heading on down to a club to do an open mic; but as I enter through the door of an building; there I can see the soldiers preparing an offense. As I ghostly got out from behind enemy line, came to a rock where as the American soldiers took aim at me, because they were unsure who I was. As I softly let them know by stating out a question, "What time is it?" and the respond was "What time is dinner?" and I reply, "It all depends who's cooking", as I proceeded pass the soldiers and down in the bunker through the door. There a general from Britain and other soldiers standing around the table looking at the map. As I approach them they all stood at attention, as I release them freely. I said: "Our enemies are preparing and are shifting in a different position and we need to step on three (3) of their position". Then the British general stated, "Even if we place our men in these positions we are still out number six hundred (600) to one (1)". So then I stated to the general, "no need to worry, I have more coming and they are waiting in the mist; about seven (7) miles from the rear and left side of our enemy". These were unique, top of the line soldiers as me. As the Chinese (Red) army about to set off the first rocket, I order the change quickly and call in the backup; as I and the two (2) soldiers left through the rear of the bunker.

After overpowering the enemy and the American celebrate, instead of heading home to have the party there, she decided that the party should be at the other house; so I agree. As I approach the other house which was only a block and around the corner; there most had on those cyclical birthday type hat. It wasn't much people in the house, as there was plenty of food. So she said to him: "More people are coming"; then he got up and stated, "I'm going to pick up a few people that just call me". I notice that his phone never rings or that he had a phone. I ask to come along, but he rejected my offer. So she says, "O.K.". Then I ask, "Were you're going?" and he replied: "To pick up a friend"; as I know he was lying. So he got up and left and got in his car. A few second later I stated to her, "I'll be back, just going outside"; as I snuck out to head to the other house; but what was so strange was if meeting someone at the house, why take the car when the house is only one (1) block away? As I approach two (2) houses away, down through the neighbor driveway and enter into the backyard, which were a setting almost like a garage or junkyard scene. As the two (2) men who were working on a car, they acknowledge me as I return back with a wave. I then head to the back of the house, looking slowly pass the driveway onto the street for the car. I then went to look on the other side; no car, but the cars that were park along the road. I walk up the step in the rear of the house and look through the glass door for any movement, so that I can enter to ensure there was no one else. I took out my keys and unlock the door, as the two (2) mechanic pass by talking among each other—hoping that they didn't think I was breaking in; as I took another look around the rear of the house toward the street, still no him or his car, but the street was getting pack with park cars. So I decided to go to the front of the house, as I slowly look for the black shiny, old Chevy Capri with dark tinted windows. As I got closer to the front, I could hear commotion. Just as I turn right, around the brushes; there he sitting on the steps as many people were coming in and out of the house. He asks, "What are you doing here?" and in shock in return I stated, "I had to pick up a couple of papers". He replies, "Really?" As he respond. "O.K., we go in to get it"; but I knew if I went in along with him, something terrible may happen. As I try to buy time to see who else I can bring along for safety; just as he got up and excuse himself to open the screen door, then she approach with two (2) of her female friends from the sidewalk asking, "No one should be here!". As she and her friends enter the house advising others to take the supplied to the other house, as I follow her in.

What's Your Interpretation?

MAY 22

Walk out down the street as being greeted by many on-lookers, as they shook and high-five me; it were like I just won some sort of election. I then went over to a building which seems like a store front; as I slip through the crowd as if someone was following me. I went into one (1) of the building to which a young man with a backpack, dropping it off to a lady, as she place the bag behind the wall. I went over to the stage and begin to talk about empowering our communities and ridden police force. As I step down off from the stage, went back to the front of the building; while standing and waiting for customers, as a black male came in, the lady hand me a small bag to which I handed over to the customer and he hand me the lump-roll up cash. After the customer left out of the building as I follow close behind, looking out through the cover-bind door, and step out three (3) step onto the sidewalk and into the car; heading down to the park where people were out partying. As I walk into a building which looks just like the building I was in, went up to the second floor to which the same woman was there as well. As she pullout another small bag and hand it over to me from a brown cabinet; as the sun begin to set. The same man came in to retrieve the package and as I hand over a clear bag seeing that it was 'grass'; but the color were like a melon forest green. As the man hand me the money and as I place the stash in my left pocket, I then turn to the woman and turn back to the man; to which he left. As he left, I saw at least seven (7) cop's cars and a few detectives vehicles with their light on; as two (2) police officer enter heading straight to the woman, as if I was invincible. Yet, worry of spending many years in prison, as the other officers head toward the building, as I began to try to slide out—to escape.

What's Your Interpretation?

_____

_____

_____

_____

_____

_____

_____

_____

_____

_____

_____

_____

_____

_____

_____

_____

_____

_____

_____

_____

_____

MAY 30

A s I walked in a house from the train station platform, down into the basement. There was a few kids trying to lure about four (4) or five (5) lizards running around the concrete floor, but it was something different about them. The color on their back was like red, as if someone was pouring hot sauce along their back; with scale grayish body. One (1) of the lizard seem like it was trying to either bite or grab one (1) of the small dog's legs; as I quickly grab a broom stick and push it near the corner. I walk back up stairs onto the platform to see if the train has come, but there were many people still waiting.

I went into a flea market type store and went to a counter waiting my turn to be serving as I held the brown leather folder in my hand underneath my left arm. As it was my turn to be served, I explaining what it is as I pull out my checkbook to make a payment. After writing out the check, I pull out another check that needed to be cash. So as I slide down the counter away from those that was standing by, as the man continually asking, "What type of product being built"; I stated, "I can't disclose that information, due to it not fully patent". So he seems to understand, as he hand me the money and ask for the check as he process the transaction. Thinking that I had already handed him the check, looked in my brown leather folder, check underneath and look back on the other counter to which it was under the package that I sat upon.

I left out from the store, through the crowd which seems to be less people; back down the stairs into the basement, which a man I respect very much, was looking around with a stick poking in between the wall and freezer, as I notice no lizards along the floor. I grab the other broom stick and poke up in the ceiling, between the wooded beam and a large lizard fell to the ground. As it slowly approach me, as I walk backward slowly up the stairs. The lizard begin to change tot a funny blue creature, whose face or mouth was of an anteater, As I hit the creature with the stick, it split in two (2) and disappear underneath the stairs; then one (1) of the kids grab hold of something. Two (2) alien (human shape) suddenly appear; the female alien tried to grab hold of one (1) of the small dogs, as if looking to eat one (1) of them, but really wanting to eat human, as she advanced to me. I grab hold of her neck to take her down. As I held her with my left hand, I felt no vocal cord or esophagus. I grab with my right hand a graham cookie with one (1) side with chocolate, which was sitting on top of a small round stool table cover with red cloth; as the alien ate her cookies. She seems to calm down and offer peace, as I pass the cookies over to the other groups to feed the male alien. As I release the alien, both went up the stairs; as a male friend and I follow close behind. I could see there were more crowd waiting along the platform, as I advised the men to keep a closed eye on them, as I looked over my left shoulder to ensure no train was coming; because the track were about two (2) to four (4) inches below the platform; which could easily jump onto the platform. As I look back to ensure he has an eye on them, and he stated, "I lost them!" and I stated, "Keep looking!"; as I look back seeing the train coming and approaching slowly. As we quickly work through the crowd and turn right down the sidewalk. As we walk by a prison-like gated apartment complex, a call out to my name as we turn and look, seeing them waving at us, as the police car pull up to the gate to get them to transport them to prison; as I stated to my friend, "Well at least we won't have to worried about prison being overcrowded".

After pasting them, we went into the building, were as my partner left to head back as he tried to convince me to come along. After entering the building, it was as if entering another dimension, where the street was dark, blue from the moon's light. In the distant I could see the bus coming and decided not to wait for the bus, so I begin to push back in the chair, I was now sitting in. I push backward and turn left and then decided it may be best to catch the bus, as I know it probably a long way back home. As I came back around the corner forward, the bus was gone. The place was dark as very few people walk the street; but now there's no one but me. I went down to the right through an opening with the chair in my right hand down the dark hallway. As I turn to go downstairs—sliding down the stair rails and another stair rail, as fast as I can; unsure what may be coming. There down a hallway something like a high school setting to which there were a few light. Saw some of the students went into their class, as the hall quickly became empty. I walk two (2) doors down and into a classroom to my right, as I see a fifteen (15) inch box T.V. on a stand; as the teacher showing the students on a fifteen (15) inch television about how to post price in the media. The ad price looked bold, numbers yet colorful as if someone did graffiti—like on the walls you see in New York. As I enter the class standing nears a female, which I notice that she was wearing a short black mini skirt, as the man next to her with his arm around across her shoulder. I begin to feel on her buttock, as the man remove his arm from around her; as I talk to her, she lean over and gave me a kiss. I turn and left out into the hallway (which were well lit) as I'm doing a cowboy dance down the hall as I enter outside, but still in the building and saw two (2) females in a cowgirl outfits in a bar which they seem to be waitress.

What's Your Interpretation?

JUNE 04— BUREAUCRAT COUNTRY

S tanding around in a gym-like setting where the room was full with known faces and new faces, as I move among the crowd as I listen to others receiving their new class schedule. As I walk over to a few of my friends, as they seem to be excited; not about the class, but new faces. As I approach one (1) of the young ladies as if I knew her and she knowing me. As she turn her back to me and back up to me close, moving up and down as I rise. I caught hold of myself to control the situation, as I back off and told her, "I see you later". I walk over to an open door to retrieve my grade reports, knowing I got an A; as I and others sat in to listen to the professor, as he teaches additional information on the Economic and finance matters, to get the country back on it feet. As I ask a few questions about taxes and what program should be look into, that is not work and how we can save to pay off the deficits. More and more students begin to enter into the room. The instructor had some valid points, as he describe on a glass-board. After showing some example, the announcer called for return students who had three (3) classes or less left to graduate, to come down to the table to receive the new schedules. So most of us got up and head back to the opening of the gym, which was still pack. As I receive my new schedule knowing the class was to be Business Law, but it wasn't. Some new subject called Bureaucrat Country, which I never heard of or know what it may hold. So then I decided if I should take the class or fight to get the class that I wanted or just drop out. Many others had the same information and went up to the administration's desk to see if it could be change or why the class were taken off, as I was still deciding.

What's Your Interpretation?

_____

_____

_____

_____

_____

_____

_____

_____

_____

_____

_____

_____

_____

_____

_____

_____

_____

_____

_____

_____

JUNE 06

As us three (3) was watching a show on T.V., as they got up in the kitchen to prepare meals for guest; he stated, "have to go to the house to check on a few things". As she ask, "To check on what?" He begin to express in a quick tone to avoid further conversation, as he left out. About a few minutes after, I let her know that I will check out to see what is really going on. As I open the glass door slowly and slip into behind the bedroom door. I could see him walking to and from reading and sending text message; minutes later, he walk over to the door and there enter a short Hawaiian looking female, as she lean up to kiss him. My first reaction was to jump out witness the incident, but I held my ground. As they walk over to a small room as I move closer into the kitchen looking behind the counter; as I snap a few pictures to send her. As he sat in a chair looking, then she begins to take her clothes off slowly. He got up to head toward the kitchen to get a drink as I move around the other side between the wall and out of sight by the square pillar. As he pour himself a drink and look around as my right foot hit up against the wall as the plate slightly shook; ignoring the sound, he headed back to the bar chair and the lady took off all her clothes, as he lean over and place a kiss between her breast. She turn around and bend over to show her inner side as he place a kiss on the 'mark'. I then try to find ways to sneak back out, as I tried to inch my way back to the door, and then the lady saw me as she turn to him. As soon as I reveal my present, the door open and she walk through seeing the action, as he know he was caught; as I prepare for an offense move.

What's Your Interpretation?

_____

_____

_____

_____

_____

_____

_____

_____

_____

_____

_____

_____

_____

_____

_____

_____

_____

_____

_____

JUNE 20

In a tunnel like train station, where there was building along the platforms. As we was on one (1) side of the river looking for ways to escape to the other side, to get over the three (3) story wall, as if someone was looking to capture us. So I advise the others four (4) or five (5) individuals, "We are making the move tonight in five (5) minutes. As we prepare, climbing over the fence. These huge seven (7) or eight (8) feet tall dark blue shadows, notice our escape over the fence. As they headed near the end of the gate to remove the lock in order to get to the other side to capture us, as we stand along the edge preparing to dive into the water. I stated to the group, "Go and I will assure to protect and see that everyone make it to the other side". As they jump into the water and seeing them swimming to the other side, without hesitation I dive in and what looked so far to get to the other side; I was able to swim ten (10) strokes, which made it seem short. One (1) female had trouble with a few strokes to get to the edge as I turn and dive underneath to support her to get closer to the edge and onto the ledge. As we climb the walls of brown crate and boxes in order to climb over the crated wall. As I got near to the top, the crates begin to loosen. As I tried to keep the crates from coming apart, I grab onto another crate in hope to grab the top of the two (2) story high wall; but as the crates begin to shake loose, I dive back into the water to which this time had a few reptiles. As I dive deeper to see where the gators or sharks was, I float straight to the top, as one (1) of the guy yell and wave for me to swim to the left and up the cardboard boxes; as they lower a rope to pull me up. As I got over the wall, I and the guys cross the track into a tunnel to retrieve items that seem to have been place for us. The ladies went down the track to see if they may have seen the light from the train. I stated, "Let get ready before the train come"; which can come at any moment and advise the ladies to be careful. As we got our bags back across the track, which the sun was up above and the ladies quickly walk back from the tunnel and onto the platform beside us; then second later the train slowly creep around the corner as it stop for us to aboard.

What's Your Interpretation?

JUNE 21

As I pull up in front of a store in a blue-purplish color pick-up truck, which seem to be an old 1967 Chevy. The dog seems to be gloomy but clear bright blue. As I enter into the hair salon shop as the hairdresser just finish the client and motion me next. I got up and sat in the chair to get my hair braided. I then notice that I didn't bring any funds nor had any cash in my pocket. Just as she unlooses two (2) braids, I wave my left hand for her to stop and mention, "I have to get some cash to which I forgot. I don't have any on me". She agrees but yet wanted to come along, which didn't make sense; which she didn't really being the process. So as I left out heading toward the truck; three (3) individuals cram in the back seat, while she and another female got in the front from the passage side. As I order all of them out, some guy name Hector complaining, "How we know he's going to get the cash?" As I responded, "It is none of your concern". As if I wanted to do something to him, but fear of being lure to the 'iron bar'. As they exit the vehicle, I ensure the small trailer was hook up to the back of the pick-up; started the truck up and head on down the street to pick up a guy named Hernandez; in which I decide not to return back to the shop. As I pull up to the front door, Hernandez, a lady, and two (2) kids got in as we head off to drop them off to their home. As we enter, Hector waiting by the door—seeming to be waiting on our arrival. As we approach the door, Hector begins to harass Hernandez about why he was hiding out, as I tried to intervene. Belling up the flight of stairs as it were wide at the bottom, but got more and more narrow at the top (sort of like a pyramid). I unlock the door which was the only door at the top of this pyramid stairs. The two (2) kids went inside as well as the woman. As Hernandez stood on the other side of the pyramid stairs, Hector tried to get pass me to either enter through the door or at Hernandez. I gave a nudge of my right elbow to Hector's stomach, as he bend forward and lost his balance falling backward down the long flight of stairs; hitting his head and back near the opening of the door. Looking down at him knowing that he would not get back up, I advise Hernandez, "I will clear the problem out and no one will know".

What's Your Interpretation?

JUNE 28

I, my father and brother enter into an open space room with a television on the left side on a table and another television behind an old style bath tub. As I saw two (2) white women in bathing suit sitting and watching something on the cube T.V. set, a show where a little white boy, who fell in a bathtub, got up in full clothes, slip and was submerge under. As the little boy climb out of the tub, as his mother grab hold of his hand, the two (2) women obtaining each other attention pointing and laughing at the crying boy. As I step in the tub, removing my shirt catching the eyes of the women in the same tub and other ladies that was sitting along the wall as they held onto their babies. A bright light shine in the middle of the room from the skylight onto an oriental rug—that is place in the center. As I sat talking to him of washing the filths and sins off me, he then hand me a red rag, which I use to wash just my feet. As I tried to inch closer to the end of the tub to move or to have some distance from the ladies that were closest to me; as he tried to bathe me as if I was a little child or to embarrass me. As I reject the help, the two (2) ladies begin to watch what was on the cube T.V's, as they focus together. As I draw closer to the ladies to see what they was zooming to, which was the same flicks of the white boy who fell in the tub got up and slip, submerging under the water as the mother yell at the boy for getting near the tub; as she lift a baby from the floated seat, as she wrap him in a towel. Then the News Report came on to report the news for the day as the two (2) white ladies laugh at the scene. As I figure it was time to get out, the water begins to float a red and blue cloud, jelly-like yet sticky, coming from underneath us, but unsure if it were coming for my penis or leg. As I stood up removing the sticky substance from between my leg and look behind me, in which 'him' was pouring a crystal clear liquid from a bottle, but the liquid split and turn red and blue as it hit the water. As I receive the towel from him not being ashamed of my nakedness, as the two (2) ladies turn and look with amazement in their eyes, while I begin to dried off my chest and back which was wet, but not while I were sitting in the tube. Then a woman came in, but she drove in a car and saw me standing as she seem to be angry for the other women getting to see me first.

What's Your Interpretation?

JULY 06

As we enter into the house, we checking to ensure that everyone was pack and ready to head over to the shelter for protection. He quickly load the SUV saying, "Let go before the news make a report in the next hour" I added, "Yes, before the highway get jam". As they got in the SUV and turn to me as I say a pray over the house and those who may be left behind—lost in sin. Then the voice stated to me, "It's time", then she say, "Are you coming?" and I stated to them, "I'll be fine. For I am protected and I will still be standing after the event". As they said, "You still can come, there's enough room". But I respond, "Don't worry, so go time is ticking" As he pull off and they look back with a smile, but worried. I got in a two (2) door coupe heading into the hardware store waiting for the announcement on the flat screen to grab the necessary items that will be needed. I had a few items in my hand waiting and standing patiently staring at the huge screen; as some look at me strange wondering why I was looking at the commercial that has been plating for months. A white man with glasses approach up to me and ask, "What are you waiting for to come on?" In replied I stated, "In thirty (30) second, be prepared to repent to enter into my Father's house". The owner of the store said, "He just crazy standing like he knows what's going to happen". Within ten (10) second, I head slowly to the door as the Special Report came on, "Everyone need to find shelter or underground as we are under attack . . . from three (3) countries which has launch a test bomb that has gone off course and is heading to the American's soil and is on the path to New York city, Boston, Dallas—Texas, Los Angeles, San Francisco, Hollywood, Disneyworld, Miami . . ." As I step out of the store as the store owner look with amazed and worry. The customers in the store begins to grab what they need; as I got in the car the street was quickly fill with cars, motorcycle, bikes and people running to and from in every directions. As I slowly drove up to the highway as many speed by, blowing their horns and some stand near under the over-path walking into an opening, as many line up hurrying themselves in. As I continue to listen to the radio; as the recording message repeat through a computer system, counting down the number of second of the impact. As I sat in the car and begin to cover myself in the materials that can take the heat wave, I crouch under the steering wheel and cover my ear and begin to ask God for forgiveness of any wrong doing I had done in the past and to have mercy on my soul; as I held my hand over my ear readying for the impact and heat. Then all of a sudden . . . 'Boom! Boom! Boom!' as the wave of heat swept across the highway designating everything in its path; as those cried out evaporate in the wind. As the heat continue to passed, I step out of the car to look around seeing people turning into dust; cars, trucks, and buses glowing red from the heat of the bomb; as I walk around observing my surrounding.

What's Your Interpretation?

JULY 09

As I stand among my friends from grade school up to college, as we all prepare for some sort of adventure or trip as if it was some sort of class reunion. Meeting and hugging each other as we head in through the gate indoor, stepping onto the down escalator as the agent took our pass or invitation card. We enter into a sanctuary talking among each other; there I see my love 'Darcel'; who I adore greatly. While I slowly pull her close to me, she said, "Something is not right" and in respond, "I got you cover and you will not be harm". As most went back up the down escalator, others choose to stay and waited for the train to come. As the train came, it was more like an open rollercoaster. As load onto the rollercoaster, the grey square box speaker of a young lady voice announce, "train is boarding, Please find your seat". As I gave her a kiss as she turn to head out and I aboard the train; obtaining my seat near the right side. As they strap the link chain across our waist, the train operator pulls the level to release the breaks. The train begins to move forward in a slow clinging jerk, as if it were picking or trying to gain momentum. The train went down a small hill and turn left, went around a slab marble wall then upward in an increasing speed, as it speed up faster and when the front of the train reach the zenith of the track, it and all the length of the train jump as if a biker would jump a ramp; going over a 'S' shape track as we landed on a small hill as I unlatch the clip to prepare to grab onto the pole, that hold the track in place. As the train increase more down the track seeing a sharp left turn, curve ahead. I stood in a low crouch position on the seat, waiting for the train to hit the curve. Just as the first two (2) cars hit, the train jump the track as it jackknife from trying to make the turn. As many fell to their death, I jump and grab onto the pole that hold up the track at a thirty-three (33) or thirty-seven (37) angle. As I swing myself down onto the solid ground, as the rest of the train wrecks piled on top of each other behind me. Then a bunch of little people in brownish-red clothing tried to grab hold of me, as I lift up in the air flying a few feet above them as they jump and reaching up in hope to grab or touch my sneaker.

What's Your Interpretation?

JULY 18

As I and a friend drove up to the school, preparing to register for class as many walk to and from, it seem to be early in the morning, because I and a few others was heading over to the cafeteria. As I walk pass a small round table, a small lamp on top with a few magazines on business, with a huge painting on the polish wall and a white man in a dark suit, bowtie with briefcase sitting as he read and prepare his study to teach the class. As I walk by, he said, "So this is your last year, Mister (Mr.) Farmer, this is it!" In replied, Yea and I'm ready". As I turn left into the cafeteria as the servers prepare the foods, as my taste for pancakes and orange juice grew.

Then heard my father was doing some work outside around the house, so my friend and I jog over down the street, passing the park across a small bridge to which only three (30 houses stood. But something tells me that I had own these houses and were to be sold, but not to my parent, because the house was not stable as it can easily be move. As I quickly grasp onto the rope to bring one (10 of the branches down, as my father saw to complete the cut. Mom in the garden planting yellow and pink dandies, as one of the neighbor came out; my mother ask, "how your father doing, how's his health", as it sound like he had a slight stroke. My father who finish what he was doing told the neighbor, "go ahead and start the grill and will show you how to Bar-B-Que. As I went over to the unstable house and step onto the right side of the porch, the house begins to lean over; as I push the house upright. But the house begin to lean again as it drop and begin to slowly slide toward the creek. As my father and friends came over to push the house away from the creek, as the tractor pull with the rope around the house. We grab many four (4) by sixteen

(16) woods to prop up the house from leaning and sliding. I told myself to remind to call the real estate agent to resale the house. As we finish stabling the house solid on the ground, my friend and I begin to prepare to head back to the college. As we walk over the bridge seeing gold fish and bright colorful butterflies, fluttering among the edge of the bridge heading down the street; which seems to be peaceful. As my friend challenge to race back to the institution, we begin jogging; talking about this is going to be a great year. As there were about five (5) to seven (7) blocks to the college; we begin to run, I begin to leave my friend behind, but I was taking small fast steps. Then I notice how quickly my friend was catching up and begin to pass me. As I tried harder, I begin to loose speed; as bystanders looks on. Then I begin to remind myself to stop or when I get myself in shape, I will be back in top form once again as soon as I stop or slow down on the drinking.

What's Your Interpretation?

JULY 31

As I enter a car dealership to test drive a few vehicles, I told the salesperson the difference between the two (2) vehicles that I had interest in. As I and the salesperson walk and discuss the issues, an young woman handed me a local newspaper; to which I just held in my hand, till another lady approach me. Then my phone begins to ring, and then I begin to receive a beep on my other phone, letting me know of a text messing coming through. I tried to stay focus on the two (2) vehicles I'm looking to choose; but something told me to read the article. As I look down at the paper and quickly turn to the front of the page and saw an article about Apostle Ron; found kill defending his family; in which they had been threaten for many years. But something came across my mind, as many continue to be ringing my two (2) phones off the hook. So then I sent out an email stating, 'We had lost a great man' and how this crime will come to justice. Then I got a call from a preacher as I look at the name on the phone caller I.D. But it only says Rev. So I answer the call and the voice was sad, slow and deep. He stated to me, "It is your time to step in, are you ready for the heat and all the pressure that is about to be upon you" and I look up to the heaven and said, "Yes, I can handle it and I'm ready to face anything, any threat that come to me". I then stated to the Reverend, "It wasn't the enemy that kill him, It were one of his college, who sent someone with no string attach to kill him. Even if we found the killer, we need to find the true source and it's one (1) of the preacher from another church".

What's Your Interpretation?

AUGUST 08

As I drove up to a parking lot to drop off a woman, who was in the passenger seat; which I assume was my wife, because I look at the steering wheel, which I saw a band of gold around my left ring finger, as she had a diamond which matches my ring. The scenery was at night with the two (2) moons shinning above in the night sky. As she lean over to give me a kiss or peck on the lip stating, "It shouldn't be long, you sure you don't want to come in?" As I respond, "No I wait out here and I'll come in a few minutes". As I watch her goes into the building, to ensure of her safety. I went to park the car, as I back the car in, got out and look back at how I park, to which look like I had park on a small bump. So I took out a remote-like device, which seems like a cell-phone with control stick. As I started up the vehicle and push the joystick forward; the car didn't respond, so I jerk the stick back and forth, the car back up an inch or two (2) and I can hear the engine roar, and took off across the parking lot. As I tried to regain control to stop the car from going, but the car would not respond as it continue till it drove up on the garbage disposable. As I was trying to wonder what is happening and fearing of what she may say when she see what just happen. Then the car backup as people ran for safety; the car move forward turning left, as I jerk the control stick and the car begin to circle around a silver-grey mini-van; squealing twice as I press continually on the stop button; then the car sped up even more as it head back toward the original parking space, but headed straight toward a SUV, which was also silver or grey color; as it demolish the vehicle, as it crash the rear end—taking the roof clearly off as the black car sat on top of the SUV. I bend down in a sitting position, placing my face in my hand saying, "What have I done . . . Why is this happening?" as she came running out as many others came to the scene. As the fire truck arrives, she says to me, "You know what you have to do now? You got to go before the cops come; I will try to hold them off". So just as I left, the police begin to arrive. As they ask questions to see what had happen, I tend to stick around at a distance to see and hear what has been stated. Then a woman came to me and told me, "You need to disappear, because they want to arrest you and put you away for life". So I left and enter a church-like building and slip through a small hole, looking at the red and blue lights. She enters through a different opening hugging me, as she stated, "Everything is going to be O.K., we just go to our other location, till things quiet down". There I held her hand as we sat and watch.

What's Your Interpretation?

AUGUST 09

E ntering in a stadium but more like a school auditorium setting; it was as if I were planning and directing for a concert. As I had a group of seven (7) individuals following and writing down how I wanted things set-up. It was to be the biggest party concert that the town will have and one (1) of the first. As the group left to get things going, I left through the side door of the stage and enter into a house like setting; to which it was more like VIP. As I gave instruction to the security what to watch for in the crowd and escape route; I and my friends head back in the auditorium, which at this time was pack with screaming crowds and cameras all over, as a Christian rock group perform in a metallic, but upbeat sound. As I got behind a female that I assume to know, and wrap my arm around her; holding her close to me. As I can feel her bottom close to my pelvis; as I raise my expectation for her to feel my needs. As we rock side to side in beat with the tune of the beat, not from the drum, but from the pluck of the strings of the bass guitar. Then one (1) of my friend came to me and stated, "There's an incident outside"; as I rub the back of her neck beneath her hairs, as I caress and place a kiss on her ear lobe; as I left to see about the situation. There two (2) females arguing over someone as one (1) of the men tried to calm the two (2) ladies down, but then the two (20 ladies begin to get in a boxing stance with hand open as they slap each other across each other faces. As the men separate the two (2) ladies as they continue to argue. I then listen in on the argument to which they were arguing over me. As they once again approach each other, I intervene just as they begin swinging wildly; which knock me backward and one (1) of the girl on my right hand side got knocks back as well. Defenseless as the other females slap violently across the face, but the effect didn't seem to slow the defenseless girl as she rose up and slap the girl back. I then order my friends to stop the fight, as they drag one (1) away to the building. I then stated, "Let go and enjoy the party". We all then head to the house that has a glass door, windows and shaded walls. As most of my friends enter, I stated, "This is for VIP and only those we closely know". A man in front of me opens the door to enter, as I excuse him stating, "This is only those on the list". I walk by to enter and turn around and saw he was from the group OutKast; I apologize, but stated, "It's an important meeting here", as many other friends enter in. As we can hear the music from the school's auditorium and seeing the event on the big embedded glass T.V. as I got behind a female and held her in my arm, as we watch the show.

What's Your Interpretation?

SEPTEMBER 02

A s I enter at a picnic setting as more and more young people gather near the long rectangle, light greyed table; as many walk on the grey square concrete slab, as if a concert were to begin; yet it was a large screen showing various artists singing and dancing as well as myself. As I had enter sitting in the back of the growing crowds in an undisclosed clothing as the five (5) men and two (2) women watched close by. A female came up to me, as I fix my shade upon my face and look down to the right of me, to which there was a gecko walking toward me; it was large, the size of a rabbit or kitten. Unsure what the gecko was about to do, in its bright lime color skin. Its craw up the wall, then leap onto my right bicep; as the lime color gecko held onto my arm, which its foot shape like a suckling cup, I then tried to shake it off . . . then tried to pull it off, as I grab the back of the gecko. The young lady that had approach me earlier, stated, "Don't hurt him"; as my bodyguard place a wood panel underneath the foot of the gecko to release the suckling foot from my right arm. I then went to sit down while a speaker came out to introduce an artist, but it was shown up on the large flat T.V's screen. As the music begin to play, I got up and start doing some crazy, yet funny dance, as I drawn the attention on me. I then notice why no one was able to reach out to me, as I continue to entertain in the VIP's room.

What's Your Interpretation?

SEPTEMBER 05

A s I enter into a home, being greeted by family's members, as everyone tend to communicating among each other's; I introduce myself and there she sat waiting for me to sit in the empty chair next to her; as if it was reserve for me. So I smoothly approach with a smile, as her smile with a twinkle in her eye. As one (1) of the member hand me a plate with steak, rice and crab legs; as we both eat off the same plate. Then many begin to leave the house, as the kids prepare their clothes for the next day. I then wave bye to her as she leave; I went in the living room to prepare a plate on the floor watching a movie. I then heard a small bang, which the sound was coming from outside; yet I kept my eyes close, and then realize my car may had been broken in and the GPS is what the thieves may take. Then there was another cranking and slamming sounds, I then decide to get up and look out the second story of the house onto the street and there was many Volkswagen Bugs about fourteen (14) or more along with a white caddy, black Infiniti, and two (2) SUV. Yet, it was early in the morning, yet still night as if it was early into the night. As I and many others step out onto the street to view the damages. I slowly approach my vehicle, assuming and expecting the damage(s); to which there was none, seeing wheels missing off all the Volkswagen Bugs. I recheck my wheels and the other vehicles to which they was O.K. I then heard some of the member—gang like talking about how much they could have got it for. So not having my cellphone in hand, I ran indoor which now seem like the house was one (1) level. I race across the living room to get to the bedroom which was a straight path in order to retrieve the phone; to make a call to the police station. But no matter how hard I ran, it seems as if I was slow in getting to the room.

What's Your Interpretation?

SEPTEMBER 06

Entering a house that seems to be gloomy, the lighting was not bright, but gave off a lavish deep purple color. As I enter into a room, which seems to be the backroom or bedroom with no bed, but a sofa and a square box T.V. On the television was a show of a beauty or swimsuit and fashion wear contest. Then a light-skinned female with a baby boy came in to see if I was going down to the show. As I feet first jump in the pool with the scuba suit on; as I rise above the water stating, "I'll be there", and submerge beneath unable to swim back up. So without panic, I sink edging near the rock walls to grab hold to lift myself back to the surface. As I notice the air-tank on my back and a smaller air-tank strap to my chest; I swam closer to the wall of the rocks and took a deep breath, as I look down at the bottomless ocean floor; yet the surface seem to be closer above. I quickly begin to float up faster and faster as I prepare to jump up onto the ground. I break through the water like a whale ascending up into the air, and landed onto the reddish-purplish carpet. Then a young man came in and asks if I was ready to go. Notice that I now have on jean, white sneaker and also dry, as I walk through the door. As we enter the arena, I walk over to the back to sit with the young ladies. Then an announcement called out, "For bathing suit contestants, please make your way to the back stage". Then a group of females that was sitting next to me as well as in front; stood up and begins to remove their clothing. However, they had their bathing suit underneath their clothing. As I reach out to a brown-chocolate female, she pull her hand from me, as she walk down the steps; in respond, "I'll be back after the contest"; as I look toward the stage, there was about nine (9) females fully clothes, as they pose and model in front of the large crowds with flashing lights.

From what I assume, it looked like it was to see who dress was best among the clothing for the church or place of worship. Then a small thin mosquito landed on my left hand, as I brush it away; which leave a mark, to which the mark begin to turn purple. Then a second purple bump appears as I grab for a solution to eliminate the pain.

What's Your Interpretation?

SEPTEMBER 14

A s I and three (3) other couples enter into a home which seem to be a getaway or summer cottage. We walk in a center like setting where many others was walking to and fro, as I went to find a seat. Then many begin to line up to aboard the buses, but I told my friends, "I'm going to stay and take on the evils". She said to me, "They are too strong, how are you going to defeat them", then I respond, "Why should we have the freedom to only come in the daytime and have to leave when the sun begin to go down? We have rights and freedoms to stay or leave at any time". As I place an oval candy cane in my mouth, trying to move it underneath my tongue; someway, somehow it ended near the back of my throat. As I tried to keep the candy from going down my throat, so I reach with my right hand to pull the candy out, as I grasp hold and carefully withdraw it from my mouth.

Then I woke up late at night and look out the window, which the other side begins separated from a stream of water and a small bridge which you can only cross over by foot. There was [those] who was trap or caged on the other side, so no humans could sneak over to free them; So I order two (2) dachshunds (long small frankfurter type dogs) to go and see how they are set up and where the rest of them were held. So the two (2) slip and slide their way through. Yet, I decided to follow behind as I order the crows to watch above and the mice to be my eyes and to setup defense. I advise the three (3) couples to keep a lookout and prepare to end this once and for all. As I cross over to the other side getting near the tree as I jump from one (1) branch to another and landed down onto the caramel grass; then the two (2) dachshunds came out with the tiger, then the mouse stated, "They set up a trap, waiting for you!"; As I turn and saw two (2) huge light pink hippo-pigs like coming out of the water as they prepare their attack; standing alongside the lion, as he gave the command to attack. I turn a little to the right and see the tiger yelling and roaring back at the lion. The two (2) hippo-pink-pigs lunge toward me as they strike me with their hoofs, knocking me back. I quickly got up and stood on top of a greyish bolder, looking to jump onto a branch to avoid and to regroup; even through the branch was slightly out of my reach. I leap forward and grasp onto the huge caramel-waffle branch and it just snap like a pretzel; as I fell toward the ground. As I sat up out of the ground, a huge graham-Chex like creature ascended; as it prepare to stand and make it attack. I stood up and order the two (2) mice to free the others and the tiger drawing onto the lion with the assistance of the dachshunds. I stood up bold and tall as I plan to strike the tall graham-Chex creature as my wings expanded.